YOU KNOW YOU'RE A CHILD OF THE

70s

WHEN...

Mark Leigh and
Mike Lepine

summersdale

YOU KNOW YOU'RE A CHILD OF THE 70s WHEN...

First published in 2004, reprinted 2006 and 2009
This revised edition copyright © Summersdale Publishers Ltd, 2011
Icons © Shutterstock
Text by Mike Lepine and Mark Leigh
All rights reserved.

Summersdale Publishers Ltd
46 West Street
Chichester
West Sussex
PO19 1RP
UK

www.summersdale.com

Printed and bound in China

ISBN: 978-1-84953-162-7

Substantial discounts on bulk quantities of Summersdale books are available to corporations, professional associations and other organisations. For details telephone Summersdale Publishers on (+44-1243-771107), fax (+44-1243-786300) or email (nicky@summersdale.com).

To.................................

From..............................

You know you're a child of the 70s when…

You begged your mum to knit you a Clanger.

If asked to name a celebrity couple, you instantly reply 'Farrah Fawcett Majors and Lee Majors'.

You close your eyes and can still taste Mint Cracknell, Amazin' Raisin and Aztec bars.

Your adolescent fantasies involved Anthea Redfern, Marie Osmond and the blonde one from Abba (and sometimes all three).

You thought the three funniest men in the whole wide world were Tim Brooke-Taylor, Graeme Garden and Bill Oddie.

You were scared stiff of
the Bermuda Triangle.

The latest advances in consumer technology always came from K-Tel or Ronco.

You used to bounce about on a spacehopper. Now you're starting to resemble one.

Your first taste of alcohol came from a lukewarm can of Top Deck shandy.

Summer holidays were
spent riding your Raleigh
Chopper and imagining
yourself as Barry Sheene
or Evel Knievel.

You once thought that the Fonz and Alvin Stardust were the hardest men on the planet.

You wouldn't go out without first checking your mood ring and your biorhythms.

You spent your childhood kitted out in clothes from C&A – if you were that lucky.

You baffle your kids by doing Frank Spencer impersonations – and then confuse them further by claiming you're 'better than Mike Yarwood' at it.

Your idea of a supermodel was an Airfix 1:72 scale B-17 Flying Fortress.

You remember being told that avocado was the new black.

You grew up wanting to be Jason King, the Six Million Dollar Man or Charlie George – if you were a boy…

… and Daisy Duke, Wonder Woman or Kate Bush if you were a girl.

You used to kid yourself that you looked like Bodie, and your best mate looked like Doyle.

You wore nail varnish, sequins and glitter – and didn't feel any less of a man for doing it.

Sophistication was pineapple and cheese on sticks and a glass of warm Cinzano.

You've never forgiven your parents for exposing you to their Roger Whittaker collection.

Men's grooming products consisted of soap on a rope, a can of Cossack hairspray and a bottle of Hai Karate or Blue Stratos.

You find yourself muttering the catchphrases 'I 'ate you, Butler', 'Nice one, Cyril' and 'Uh-Oh Chongo'.

Your idea of an 'illegal download' was taping songs off the radio with a handheld microphone.

You resented the fact that everyone was on strike except schoolteachers.

You can still play 'Stairway to Heaven' on your tennis racket.

You remember reading the chess results in the sports pages of national newspapers.

A 'home cinema system' consisted of a Super-8 projector and a white sheet.

The biggest decision you ever had to make was 'Donny Osmond or David Cassidy?'

You were a member of the official *Planet of the Apes* fan club and the KISS Army.

You still occasionally craving a bottle of Cresta ('It's frothy, man!').

You spent a month with your wrist in plaster after a horrific Klackers accident.

You think Dick Emery made a more convincing woman than David Walliams.

You put your atrocious spelling down to all those Slade song titles.

Having G-Plan furniture,
wall-to-wall carpeting,
a yucca plant and a
through lounge confirmed
that your family were
middle class.

Your dream car was a Ford Capri 2000 XL. That or a Lunar Roving Vehicle.

You looked forward to watching *Ask the Family* and identifying the close-up black and white photo of a comb or a pencil sharpener.

You used to wear tartan
– and you'd never even
been to Scotland.

You once started each day with a bowl of Puffa Puffa Rice or Golden Nuggets.

You'd spend hours in Miss Selfridge discussing the various merits of baggies, parallels, bell-bottoms or flares.

You remember 'cod wars' and your parents reassuring you that Iceland would never resort to 'the nuclear option'.

All your pocket money was spent on Pink Panther bars, Bazooka Joes and *Countdown* comics.

You not only know what carbon paper is, but you used it regularly in your first office job.

You could once enthral
30 classmates just by
showing off your
new Blakeys.

Marc Bolan and his feather boa got you all confused about your sexuality... at just the wrong time of life.

There was a universally and socially understood jeans hierarchy: Levis, Wranglers, Lee, Brutus Gold... then Keynote.

You can't quite convey to your children just how good a Lord Toffingham ice lolly tasted.

You managed to sneak in, underage, to see *The Exorcist* – and then spent many sleepless nights wishing you hadn't.

You and your friends had a gang based around *The Tomorrow People.*

The children's TV presenters were as old as your dad, not your big brother.

You'll never forget the day the Phantom Flan-Flinger attacked the St Winifred's School Choir on *Tiswas.*

You don't consider dark brown and cheesecloth to be crimes against fashion.

TV ad breaks regularly featured useful public information films warning you about the perils of playing near railway lines and accepting lifts from strangers.

You think Queen's 'Bohemian Rhapsody' is the greatest pop video ever made.

You attribute your short-term memory loss to all the chemicals in the Parma Violets you scoffed down back then.

You and your mates all had a favourite 'angel' from *Charlie's Angels* and you'd spend hours arguing who was the tastiest.

Your child's weekly
pocket money is more
than your first weekly
pay packet.

You wished you could be adopted by the Partridge family.

Staying in a half-built hotel in Magaluf or Benidorm was considered exotic.

The most powerful computer in your home was an Atari 2600 with 128 colours.

You really believed that
Gary Numan was radical,
avant-garde and rebellious.

You once thought that the sight of Terry Scott dressed as a schoolboy was funny (and not deeply disturbing).

You can sing the words and perform all the actions to 'The Lumberjack Song'.

All the clothes you wore back then (and your haircuts) can now be found on humorous birthday cards.

You could always count on your best friend's mum to give you a glass of warm, semi-flat Tizer.

You remember a peanut farmer being elected president… and thinking the Americans couldn't get any more ludicrous than that.

You were genuinely shocked when you found out where pop group 10cc got their name from.

You thought you laughed out loud at *The Two Ronnies*. Now, seeing re-runs of the show, you realise you must have been mistaken.

You sometimes get the urge to put your fingers in your belt loops and do the 'Tiger Feet' dance.

A rite of passage was heralded by changing from *Beezer* and *The Dandy* to *Corr!!* and *Whizzer and Chips*.

Being taken to a Wimpy bar was seen as a treat.

You used to have a cassette of *Derek and Clive* that you kept hidden from your mum.

You tell anyone who'll listen that Karl Douglas could kick Jackie Chan or Jet Li's butt.

You find yourself scouring eBay for that elusive 1970s World Cup Squad coin collection or *The Sun*'s football stamp album.

You think radio peaked with *The Kenny Everett Show* and the genius that was Captain Kremmen.

You begged your dad to paint a white stripe down the side of his Mk III Cortina, so that you could both play at being Starsky and Hutch.

The biggest, most bad-ass rappers you'd ever seen were the Sugarhill Gang.

You never could quite work up the nerve to push a safety pin through your nose, but you knew you were a punk at heart.

You're still trying to figure out what 'Can the Can' was all about.

Somewhere, in a safely guarded keepsake box, is your 'Rock Against Racism' badge.

You know that Tavares is
NOT a tropical disease.

Only the most middle class of your schoolmates' parents ever served up butterscotch Angel Delight.

You can't believe you were ever engrossed in a soap opera about a North Sea ferry starring Kate O'Mara.

You still maintain that there was nothing wrong with queuing for eleven hours to see *Star Wars*.

All the great songs of your childhood are readily available on free CDs with the weekend newspapers.

THANK YOUS

From Mike:

Philippa Hatton Lepine

From Mark:

Debbie, Polly and Barney

Mike Lepine

Mike Lepine spent his formative teenage years in the 1970s and – despite the constantly changing fashions – couldn't fit in with any of them. He had no gender identity issues to work out with Glam, was far too reactionary for Prog, had absolutely no funky stuff whatsoever to strut during the 'difficult' Disco Years and thought that wearing a bin bag and gobbing at people was just another boring way of conforming. He did like those big Super Mousse chocolate bars, though…

Mark Leigh

Born in 1966, Mark Leigh grew up in the 1970s wanting to be the lead guitarist in Slade, the pilot of Skylab or the Fonz. He has vivid memories of a weird TV series called *HR Pufnstuf* but doesn't know if this really existed, or was just a hallucination from eating some out of date Spanish Gold sweet tobacco. Mark used to have fantasies about Olga Korbut, Ruth from Pan's People and Susan Stranks, and, if truth be known, still does.

www.summersdale.com